Kirstine Nikolajsen and Inge Lise Nil

Tatting - Just knots

Tatting for beginners

Akacia

Drawings by Kirstine Nikolajsen
Photos by Jan Illum Marcussen
Printed at Øko-Tryk I/S, Videbæk, Denmark

ISBN: 87-7847-050-1

Introduction

Tatting is just knots; knotted on a thread and pulled together to make rings and chains. The system and materials are simple, but it is perhaps that, which makes tatting into a fascinating needlework. The description of ‚Poor mans crochet‘, ‚The unnecessary needlework‘ and ‚Luxury needlework‘ has throughout time been attributed to tatting, but in spite of the description, it has become a timeless needlework with many possibilities.

In February 1994 we published the book „Tatting“ (published by NOTABENE) with 52 patterns in classical tatting, that is to say all the work was tatted in crochet yarn and used for edging, doilies, bridal crowns to name some examples. The book gave precise instructions of the tatting technique and all the patterns were shown as visual patterns.

This book „Tatting - Just knots“ is planned as a book for beginners of all ages. The book describes the basic techniques of tatting - also for left handed people - and there are instructions for all 41 patterns. The patterns are worked out with easy to follow diagrams, and a short description where we found it necessary.

We have tatted the classical designs in different yarns and colours, which have given possibilities for untraditional uses. For example bandeau's in knitting cotton and earrings in gold and silver thread.

The book also has a chapter about creative tatting. Creative tatting differs from classical tatting with the use of reverse knots to create chains and stalks in flower designs. This gives possibilities to tat with several tatting shuttles and to still reach a complete result! The motifs are useful for decoration on cards, in key rings and so on. All the patterns in the book are small and technically simple for beginners to work.

We have attempted to inspire you with many different and exciting uses/possibilities for tatting but it is only the imagination which can limit the possibilities for tatting.

Good tatting.

The possibilities are innumerable - The pleasure inexhaustible.

The Materials

Before you start, you should obtain some tatting shuttles in different colours, a delicate crochet hook to use for joining. In some patterns, paper clips are used to create a little space in the middle, and a pair of tweezers is a good tool to have if you make a mistake and it is necessary to open a ring. A pair of scissors is necessary for cutting ends off the yarn.

Finally you require yarn to tat with. The yarn needs to be firm and smooth so that it slides easily, but at the same time it needs to be strong so that you can pull the knots together to form a ring without the thread breaking.

In this book we have used crochet yarn and metal yarn from D.M.C., and also Mercer Knitting cotton from Jacobsdal.

All of the requirements can normaly be found in needlework shops.

Pattern Description

For each design we have given the requirements, yarn and measurements. Every pattern is worked out as a visual pattern with a short explanatory text. Often it is only part of the design which its drawn, but it will be shown by photograph and text how the pattern should be repeated and joined.

The second thread is taken directly from the ball. By omitting to cut the thread when the yarn is wound around the shuttle, we can then avoid frayed knots at the beginning of the work.

Explanation of symbols

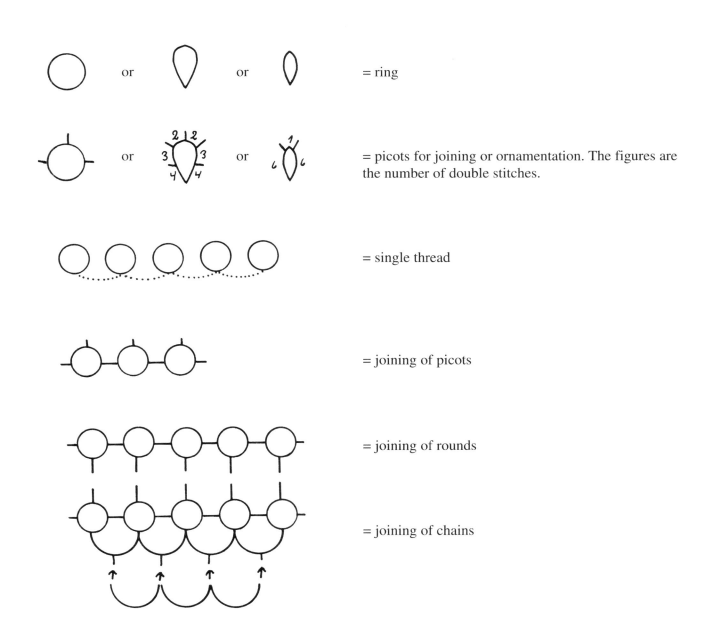

or   or   = ring

or   or   = picots for joining or ornamentation. The figures are the number of double stitches.

= single thread

= joining of picots

= joining of rounds

= joining of chains

 = lock stitch

⊗ = Josephine knot

▷ = place to put in a paper clip either at the start of the work or to make an interval between the stitches

—⊖ = picot or string with beads

 = A B C D E succession of rings
a b c d e succession of chains

 = repetition of design

〜〜〜 = Spiral cord. Made of half double knots tatted on the ball thread. When the knots are pulled tight together the cord will become a spiral.

Technique

Tatting knots consist of two half knots, a left half and a right half. Together they make a double stitch.

The left half of the knot

Figure 1

Place the thread around the left hands finger tips and keep it firm with thumb and forefinger, but not firmer than the thread can slide between the fingers. The middle finger and the third finger, as the thread are placed around must be able to pull the thread to increase the dimension of the loop.

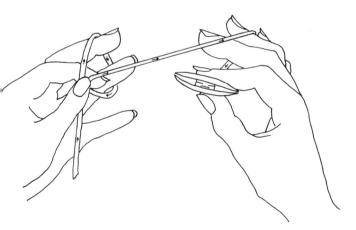

Figure 2

Make a loop with the shuttle <u>under</u> the left hand thread.

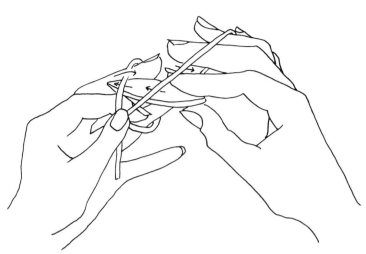

Figure 3

Release the grip in the left hands middle and third finger and pull the shuttle. This makes the loop transfer to the other thread. Keep the thread in the shuttle firm and pull the knot down between thumb and forefinger with the help of the left hands middle finger.

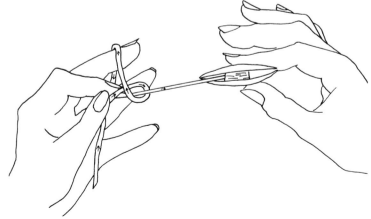

The right half of the knot

Figure 4

With the shuttle make a loop over the left hand thread. Release the grip in the left hand and pull the tatting shuttle, transferring the knot in the same way as with the left half of the knot.

Figure 5: Picot

A picot is a shorter or longer space between two double stitches and is used for ornamentation and joining.

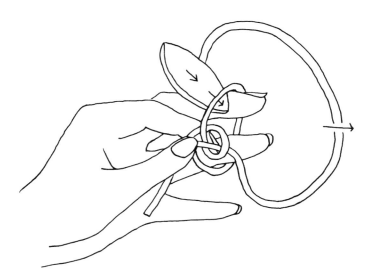

Figure 6: To close a ring

Work a series of double stitches and when the desired number of double stitches are tatted, pull the tatting shuttle and the knots become a ring.

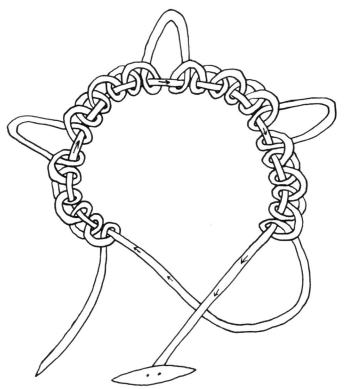

Figure 7: The opening of a ring

The correction of a mistake in tatting; a ring can be opened at a picot, after which the inner thread can be pulled with a pair of tweezers.

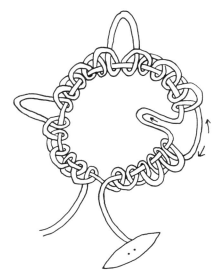

Figure 9: Chains

Chains are made with thread directly from the ball.
When the ring is made, turn the work around and work the chain with the thread from the ball.

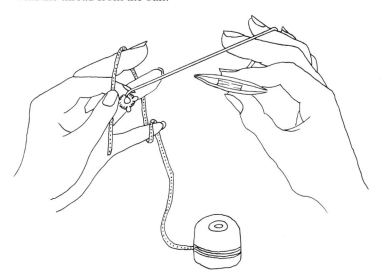

Figure 8: Joining

The thread is pulled through a picot with the help of a crochet hook.

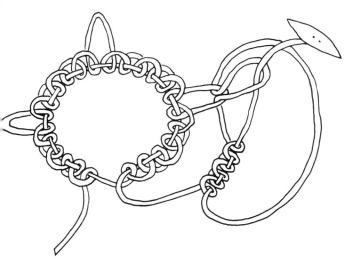

Figure 10: To join a chain

The thread is pulled through a picot with the help of a crochet hook.

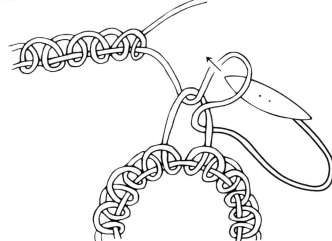

Figure 11: The addition of a motif

The finished work folds over backwards to the left, the picot on ring A is turned around and afterwards joined as normal.

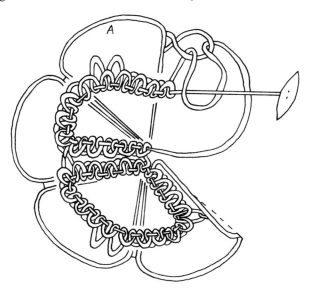

Figure 13: Reverse knots

A reverse knot is a double stitch, but the loops are made with the thread from the tatting shuttle. This means that the knot closes the work and cannot be pulled, it can only be used in chains with the thread from a ball.

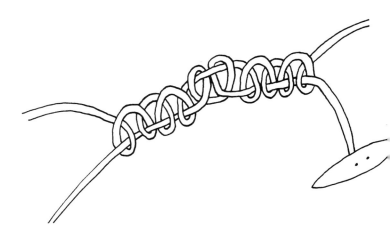

Figure 12: Renewing the thread or completion of the work

The knots shown - in this book described as frayed knots - are tied tightly to each other and the ends cut off.

Figure 14: Josephine knot

A Josephine knot is made up of half stitches pulled together to form a ring.

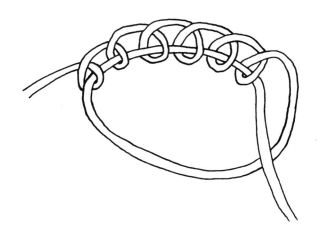

The technique for left handed people

The left half of the knot

Figure 1A

Place the thread around the right hand's finger tips and keep it firm with thumb and forefinger, but not firmer than the thread can slide between the fingers. The middle finger and the third finger, which the thread is placed around, must be able to pull the thread to increase the dimension of the loop.

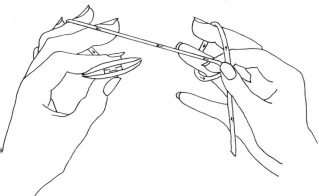

Figure 2A

Make a loop with the shuttle <u>under</u> the right hand thread.

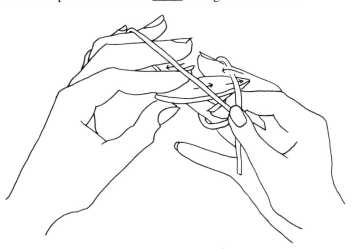

Figure 3A

Release the grip in the right hand's middle and third finger and pull the shuttle. This makes the loop transfer to the other thread. Keep the thread in the shuttle firm and pull the knot down between thumb and forefinger with help of the right hand's middle finger.

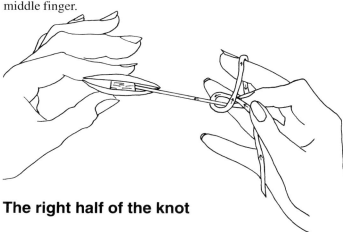

The right half of the knot

Figure 4A:

With the shuttle make a loop over the right hand's thread. Release the grip in the right hand and pull the tatting shuttle, transferring the knot in the same way as with the left half of the knot.

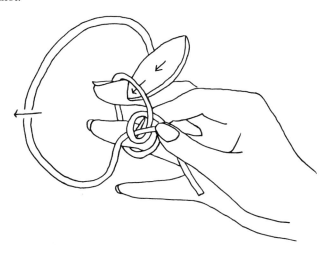

Diagram for hairnet.

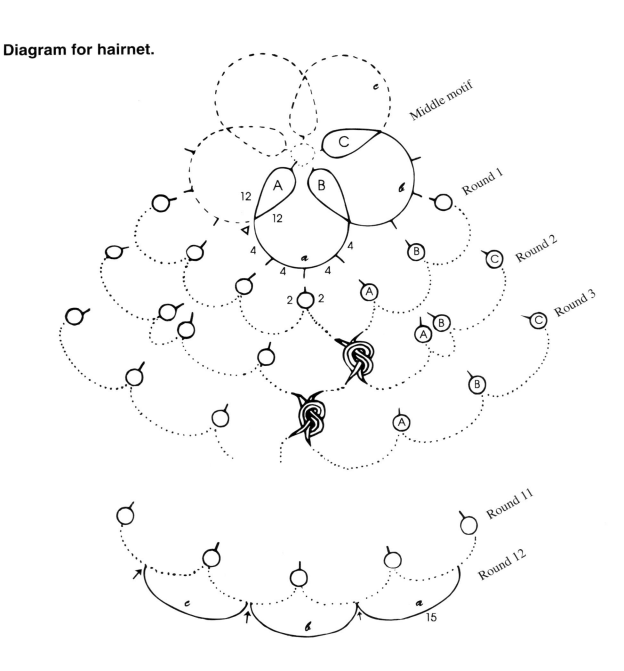

A small hairnet for a bun

Materials: 1 shuttle + ball thread
                 Sateen ribbon 0.6 cm wide, 75 cm long
Thread: DMC Pearl Cotton No. 50, colour 115 red merle

First tat the inner motif, finish with frayed knots and cut the ends. The first round is started with shuttle and ball thread. The thread from the ball is used for the knots, which joins the rounds (see the diagram). The single threads between the rings in rounds 1-11 should be approximately 2 cm in length. Rounds 3-11 are the same. Round 12 is only chains tatted with the ball thread. The satin ribbon is pulled through the chains.

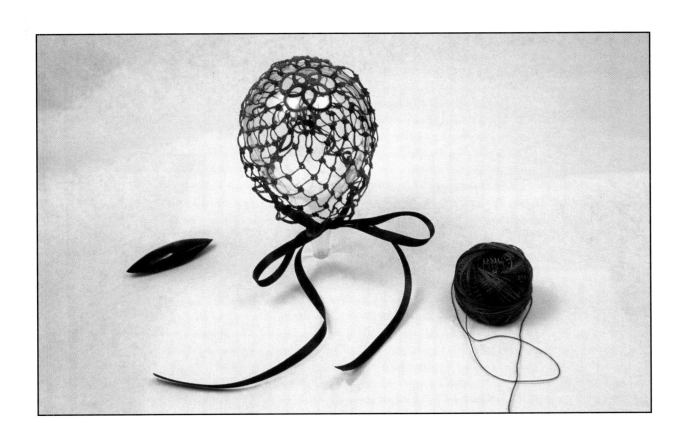

Bandeau and bracelet in thick yarn

Bandeau:

Materials: 1 shuttle + ball thread
22 beads app. 7 mm in diameter.
15 cm round elastic
Thread: Jacobsdals „BAHAMAS" knitting cotton
Size: length app. 30 cm
width app. 4 cm

The bandeau is made of 22 rings.
Remember to pull the beads forward and place them in the picots. The bandeau is formed into a ring and finished with frayed knots. Pull the elastic through the picots on the rings.

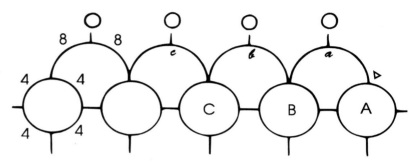

Bracelet:

Materials: 1 shuttle + ball thread
11 beads
Thread: Jacobsdals „BAHAMAS" knitting cotton
Size: length app. 20 cm
width app. 4 cm

The bracelet is made of 11 rings.

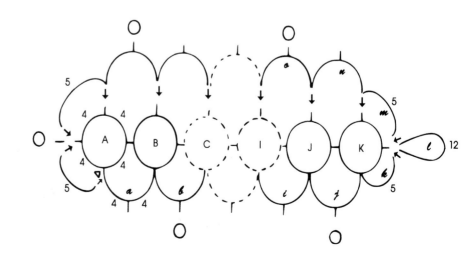

14

15

Flower for hairband

Materials: 1 shuttle + ball thread
                   „Stamen" with beads
                   1 hairband covered with fabric
Thread: DMC Cordonnet Special No. 30, colour white

Crochet the tips together using double crochet and form the flower around the stamens.Sew the flower onto the hairband.

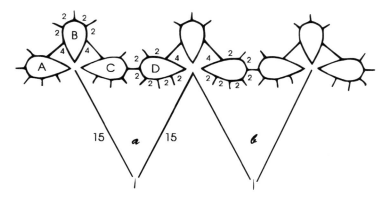

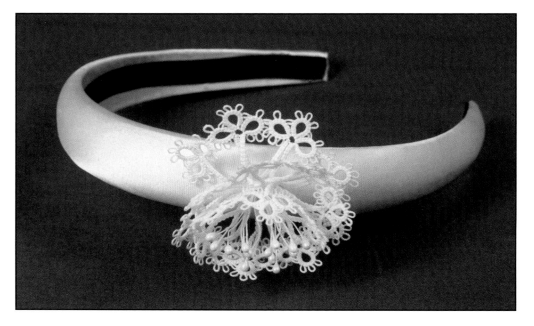

16

White bandeau with cross

Materials: 1 shuttle + ball thread
                Sateen ribbon 0.6 cm wide, 75 cm long.
Thread: DMC Cordonnet Special No. 20, colour white

Start to tat at chain *a*.

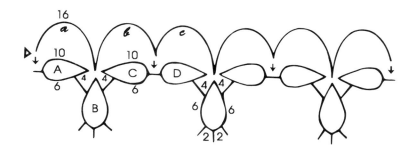

Diagram for white hair net

White hair net for a bun

Materials: 1 shuttle + ball thread
                  Sateen bandeau 0.6 cm width, 75 cm long.
Thread: DMC Cebelia No. 10, colour white

First tat the centre motif. Each round is tatted separately and concluded with a frayed knot.

Black necklace and bracelet with Greenland beads

Materials: 1 shuttle + ball thread
                    34 Greenland beads for the bracelet
                    2 small buttons
Thread: DMC Cordonnet Special No. 20, colour 310 black
Size: necklace app. 31 cm long, 1.5 cm wide
                    bracelet app. 13 cm long, app. 2.5 cm wide

Start the work at ring A. Tat the first 9 double stitches in the last chain (the button chain), then cut the ball thread leaving app. 60 cm on the work. Pull the thread through the button hole 3 times and then tat the last 9 double stitches. Finish with a frayed knot.

The necklace is made of 35 rings or until the desired length is reached.

The bracelet is made of 18 rings or until the desired length is reached.

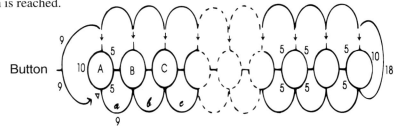

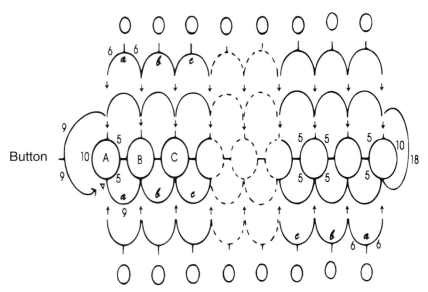

20

21

Oval bracelet with beads

Materials: 1 shuttle + ball thread
             1 little button
             30 beads, 5 mm in diameter
Thread: DMC Cordonnet Special No. 20, colour 210 light lilac
Size: width at the middle 4 cm
             length app. 14.5 cm

Start the work at ring A. The large arrows on the diagram show the middle of the bracelet. For how to mount the button see the „Black necklace and bracelet with Greenland beads" page 20.

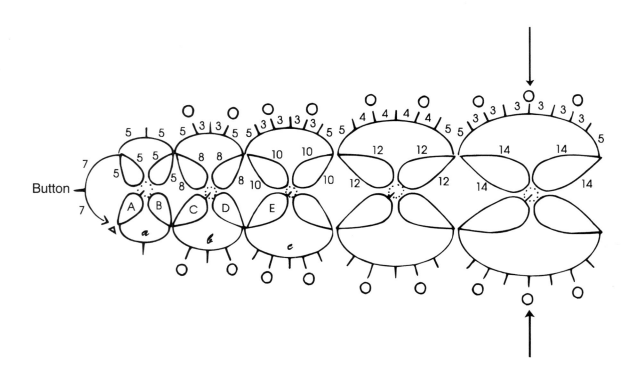

22

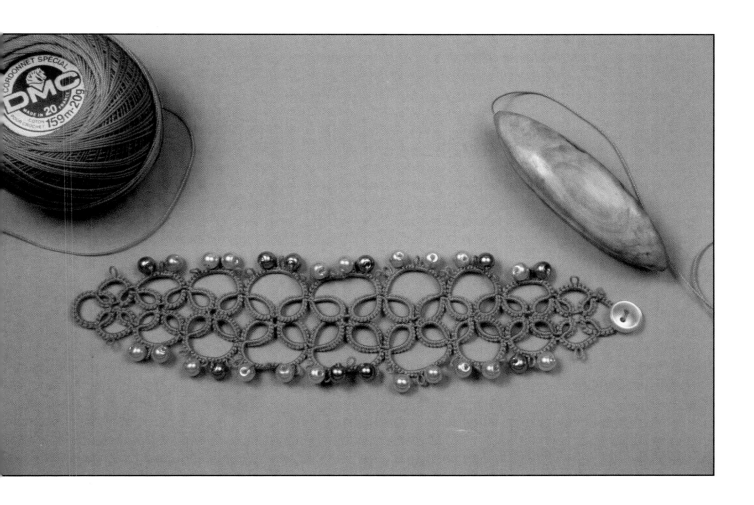

Candle guard tatted on ring

Materials: 1 shuttle + ball thread
                1 plastic curtain ring 3.5 cm in diameter
Thread: DMC Cordonnet Special No. 50, colour white

To tat around a ring it is necessary that the ring is large enough to allow the shuttle to pass through. The thread should be placed around the ring as shown in the working diagram.
On the ring there are 29 picots plus the joining to the beginning thread. Don't cut the thread but let it continue in the 1st round, which is made of 30 chains.

Working sketch:

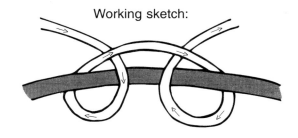

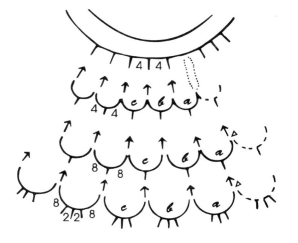

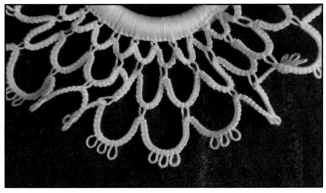

24

Hairband with flowers

Materials: 1 shuttle
                8 golden beads 4 mm in diameter
                1 hairband covered with fabric
Thread: DMC Cordonnet Special No. 40, colour white
Size: 2.5 cm in diameter

Tat 8 flowers.
Sew gold beads to the hair brace and ‚button' the flowers on the pearls. If necessary
sew the flowers with invisible stitches.

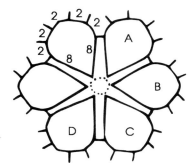

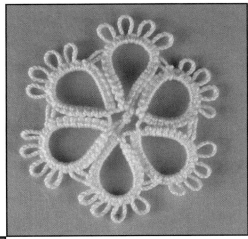

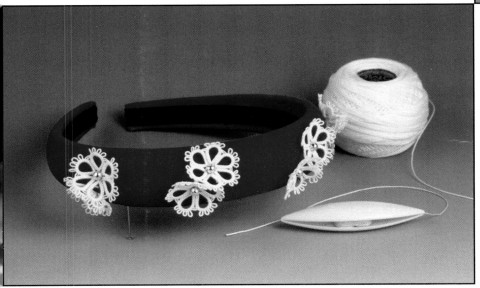

Trimmings for T-shirt

Materials: 1 shuttle
Thread: DMC Cordonnet Special No. 20, colour 666 red
Size: the chain is 1.5 cm wide
               the water lily is 3.5 cm in diameter

The working diagram shows how to get from one pair of leaves to the next. The thread between the pairs measures 2-3 mm.
The bottom of the water lily - i.e. the large flower - is tatted first. When the flower is finished: tie the beginning thread and the thread from the shuttle to each other but don't cut the ends. Start the little flower on top of the large one as shown on the working diagram.
Note that there are 6 spaces in the little flower and 9 spaces in the large, when joining leave every third space open.

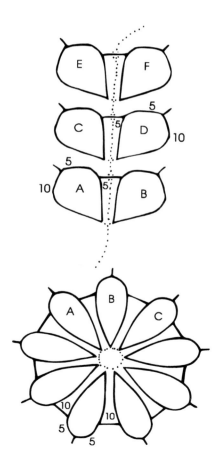

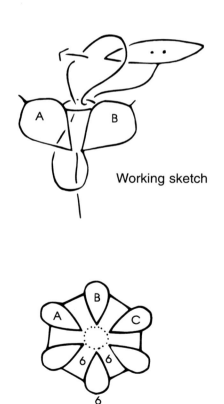

Working sketch

26

Earring in gold thread

Materials: 2 shuttles
                1 pair of earring wires or clips
Thread: DMC Fil Or clair, Art. 282 gold
Size: 5 cm x 2.5 cm

Wind thread on 2 shuttles in such a way that there is a shuttle at each end of the same thread.
First tat ring A.
Next tat the rings B with each shuttle. Twist the threads between the pairs of rings and ensure that each shuttle works down one side.

Earring in silver thread

Materials: 1 shuttle
                1 pair of earring wires or clips
Thread: DMC Fil Argent clair, Art. 283 silver
Size: diameter 2.5 cm

The pattern is the same as on page 25.

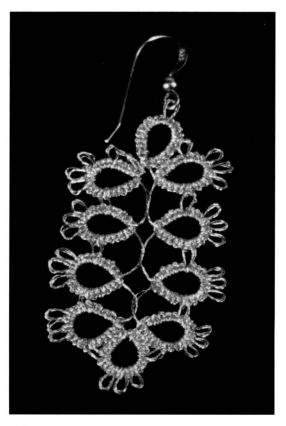

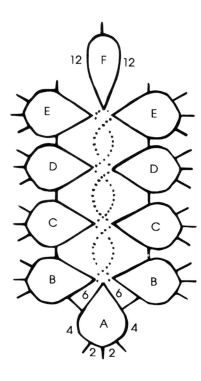

Candle guard for Easter

Marerials: 1 shuttle + 1 ball thread
Thread: DMC Pearl cotton no. 8, colour 90 yellow merle
Size: diameter app. 8 cm.

The outside round is made of chains.

Easter egg

Materials: 1 shuttle + ball thread
              polystyrene egg 6 cm
Thread: DMC Cordonnet Special No. 40, colour 3326 pink

Tat 2 four-leaf clovers and a band made of 16 rings. Close the band to a ring and place it around the egg. Keep the ring and the four-leaf clovers on the egg with pins. Join the picots on the clover and the ring by using the thread from the shuttle. Fix the thread in each picot as shown on fig. 10 page 9. When you have worked all the way around the clover the band is pulled in shape and covers the egg.

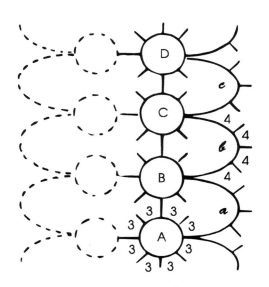

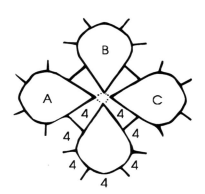

30

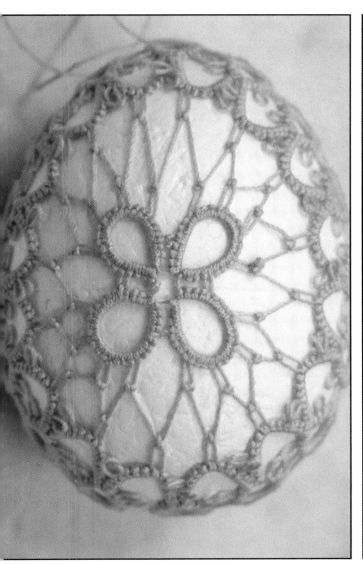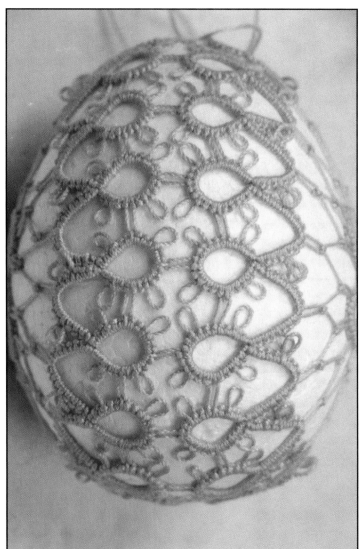

31

Ornament for candlestick

Materials: 1 shuttle + ball thread
Thread: DMC Pearl cotton No. 8, colour 3 1 1 dark blue
Size: 3.5 cm in diameter

First tat both centre motifs. Don't cut the thread after last motif. Continue with the spiral cord made solely by half stitches. When the cord measures app. 50 cm tie it to the second motif.

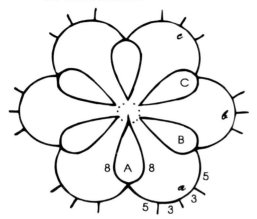

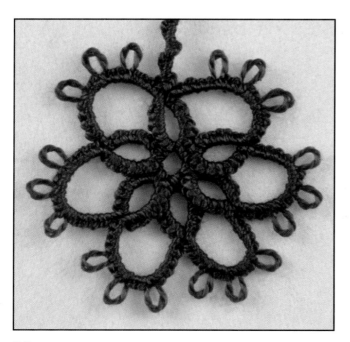

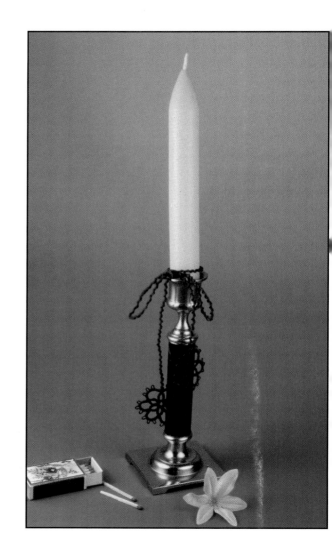

Napkin ring with beads

Materials: 1 shuttle + ball thread
                 36 small glass beads
Thread: DMC Cordonnet Special No. 40, colour white
Size: width 2.5 cm

Band made of 9 motifs closed into a ring.
The band is made of 2 rounds.
Remember to pull the beads forward and place them in the picots.

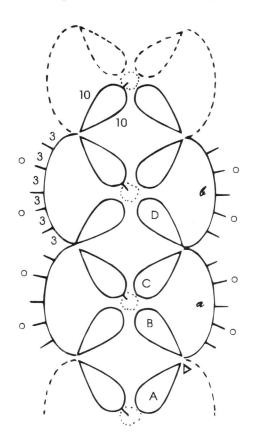

Lace for handkerchief

Materials:	1 shuttle + ball thread
	1 handkerchief with hemstitch 20 x 20 cm
Thread:	DMC Cordonnet Special No. 60, colour white
Size:	lace width app. 1.7 cm

On a 20 cm handkerchief there are room for 15 trefoils on each side. Measure out and put pins at the edge for each app. 1 .5 cm. Mark the places with a lacking-thread and remove the pins.
Tat the lace according to the visual pattern and join it to the handkerchief at each mark.
Joinings are made as usual: pull the thread through a hole in the hem by use of a crochet hook, and push the shuttle through the produced loop.

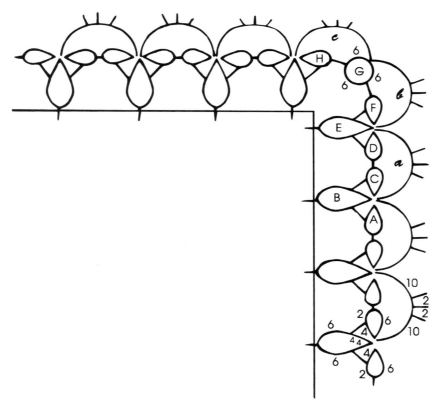

Bookmark - cross

Materials: 1 shuttle + ball thread
Thread: DMC Cordonnet Special No. 60, colour white
Size: 5 cm width
              8.5 cm long
              the cords measures 2.5 cm and 3 cm

The centre motif is tatted first. The picots have to be short.
Place a paper clip at the start of ring A.

The rings and the chains in the clovers have the same
number of double stitches as in the cross.
The cords are made as spiral cords in continuation of the
first motif. Place a paper clip after the spiral cord and
continue with ring B without cutting the thread.

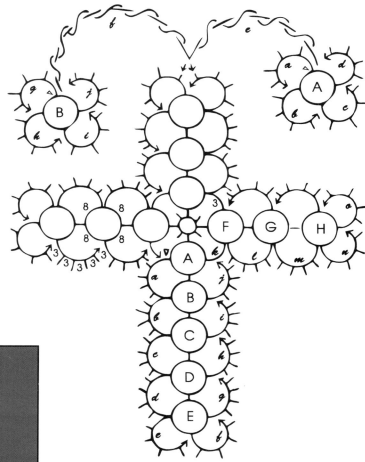

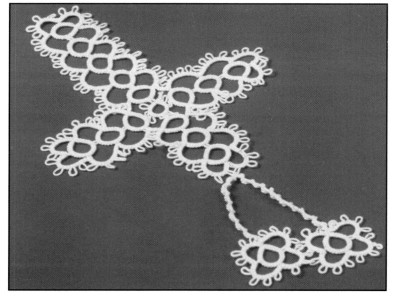

Centre motif: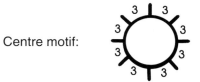

36

Christmas basket made of 5 squares

Materials: 1 shuttle + ball thread
Thread: DMC Cordonnet Special No. 30, colour 666 red
Size: each side measures 3.5 x 3.5 cm

The baskets are made of 5 squares joined as shown in the
diagram. The handle is made of 11 rings.

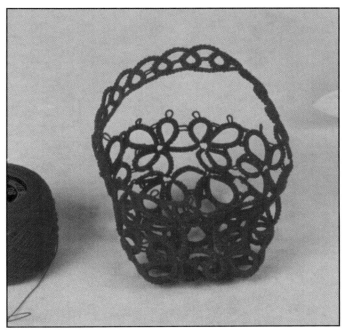

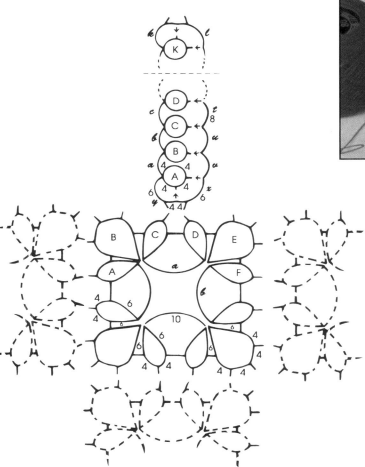

Square doily

Materials: 1 shuttle + ball thread
Thread: DMC Cebelia No. 30
                  the rings: colour 743 yellow
                  the chains: colour 699 green
Size: 21.5 x 51.5 cm

The doily is tatted in 2 halves. Each half is 7 chains wide. When the desired length is reached tat the chains with the 3 picots, and continue the row so that the second half is started, and the doily reaches its full size. Tat the second half of the doily in the same way and join it down the middle at the arrows.

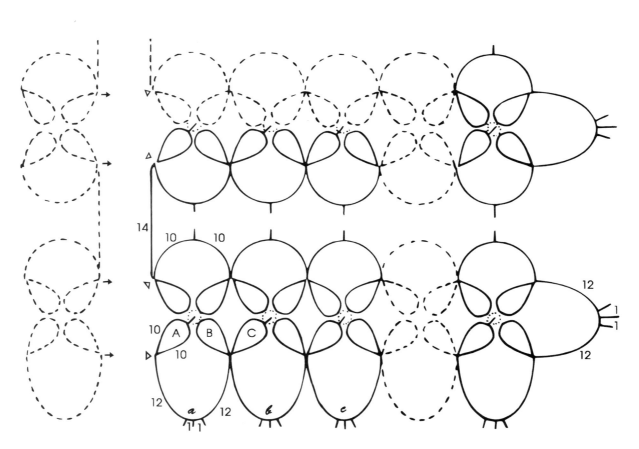

38

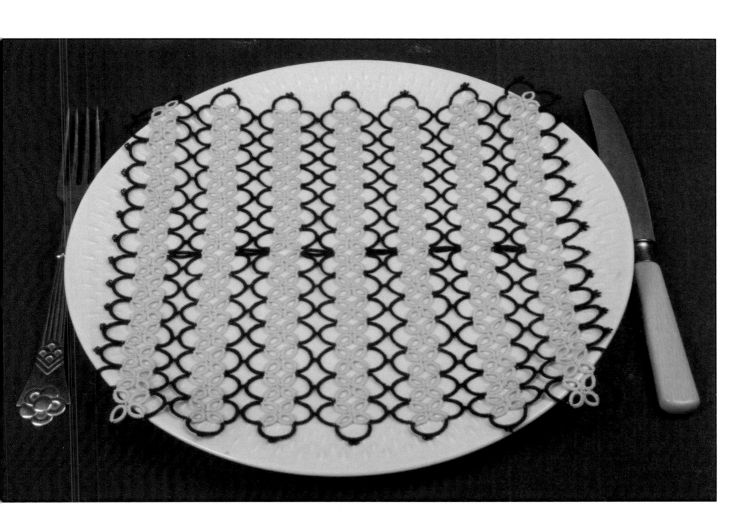

Bookmark

Materials: 1 shuttle + ball thread
Thread: DMC Cordonnet Special No. 50, colour white
Size: app. 4 cm wide
    app. 11 cm long
    the cords measure 5.5 cm and 6.5 cm

Bookmark made of 3 joined motifs.
The cords are tatted as chains by using the ball thread. The desired length of the cord is determined by the number of double stitches.

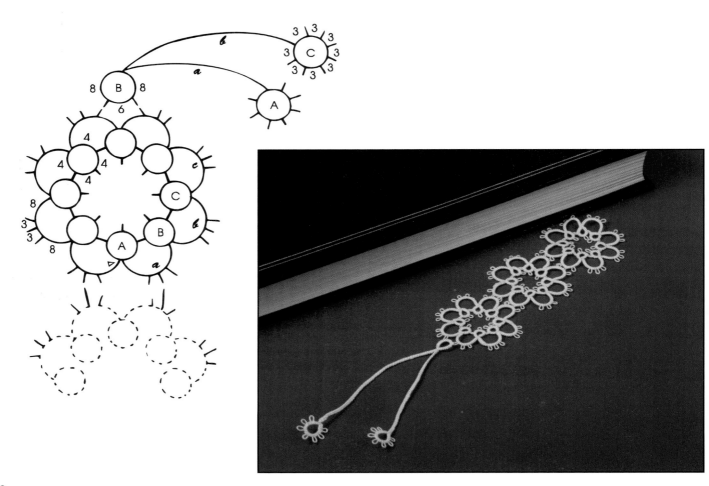

Christmas heart

Materials: 1 shuttle + ball thread
Thread: DMC Cordonnet Special No. 20, colour 666 red
Size: 3 x 3 cm

At the end of the work join chain *e* to the trefoil and then tat the handle as spiral cords in the desired length.

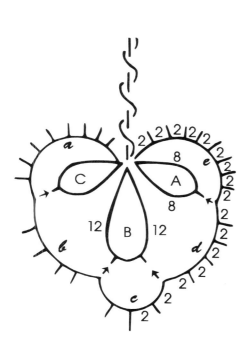

Hair bow

Materials: 1 shuttle
                     fabric for the bow
                     1 hair slide
Thread: DMC Cordonnet Special No. 60, colour white
Size: the width of the lace is app. 0.75 cm

Sew a bow of two pieces of fabric and turn them inside out. Pleat it on the middle as shown at the diagram and fix if necessary to keep it in shape.
Tack the lace to the edge. Make a band of fabric app. 2 cm width and app. 7 cm long.
Tack the double lace to the band, and sew it around the middle of the bow.
Sew the bow to a hair slide.

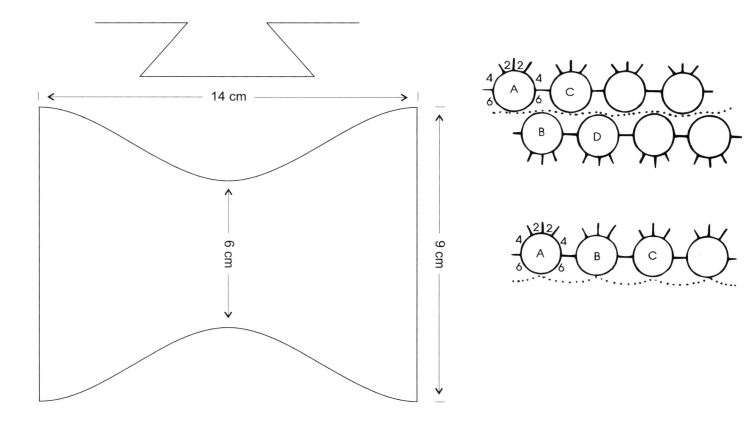

Motif for key ring

Materials: 1 shuttle + ball thread
                    1 key ring with plastic pendant 4 cm in diameter
Thread: DMC Cordonnet Special No. 40, colour white
                    DMC Fil Or clair, Art. 282 gold
                    Size: 2.8 cm in diameter

First tat the centre motif. The outer round is tatted as chains.

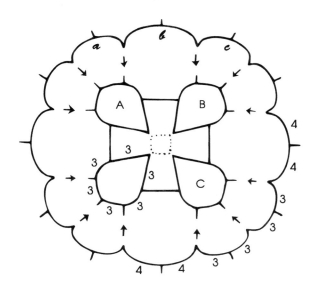

44

Lace for hair scrunchie

Materials: 1 shuttle
Sateen ribbon 60 cm long and 6 cm wide
flat elastic app. 20 cm
Thread: DMC Cordonnet Special No. 20, colour 799 blue
Size: the lace: 1 cm wide, 60 cm long

Stretch the elastic and sew it to the middle of the sateen band. Close the band into a ring and fix the ends with a few stitches. Tack the lace to the edge with a thin sewing thread.

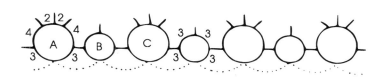

Lace for handkerchief

Materials:	1 shuttle + ball thread
	1 piece of linen 25 x 25 cm
Thread:	DMC Cordonnet Special No. 50, colour
Size:	diameter 5 cm

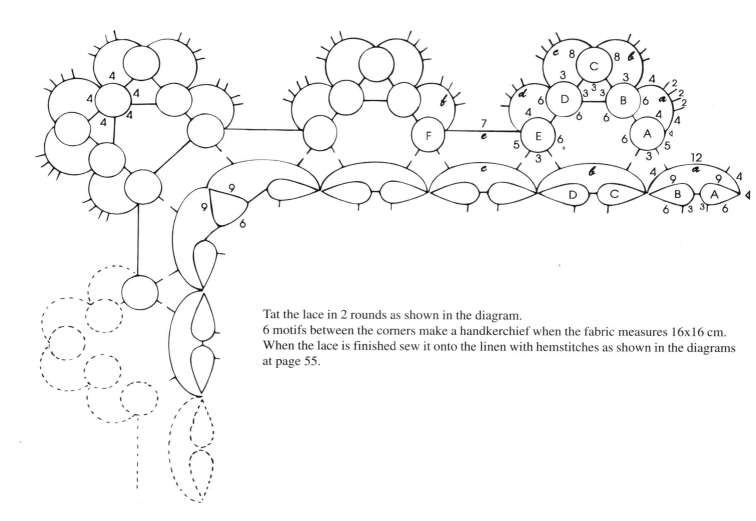

Tat the lace in 2 rounds as shown in the diagram.
6 motifs between the corners make a handkerchief when the fabric measures 16x16 cm.
When the lace is finished sew it onto the linen with hemstitches as shown in the diagrams
at page 55.

Heart for keyring

Materials: 1 shuttle + ball thread
                  1 keyring with heart shaped plastic pendant
Thread: DMC Fil Argent clair, Art. 283 silver
Size: the motif measures 3.5 cm in height

Remember to join the chains in the picots on ring C and A.

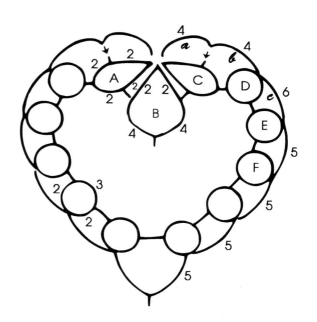

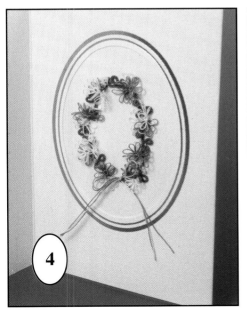

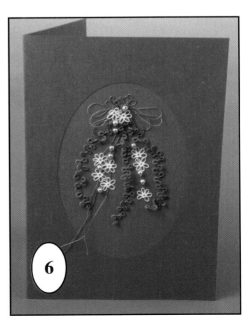

49

Creative tatting

In creative tatting imagination and creativity have a free hand. You can tat flower motifs and stalks without using any established pattern, it is completely up to oneself, what the finished result should be. The motifs are very suitable for card decorations, in key rings, for hair accessories, and anything else that you can imagine, but on the whole one must say creative tatting should not be washed, the single threads and long picots cannot stand it.

Creative tatting demands a special technique - see the diagram.

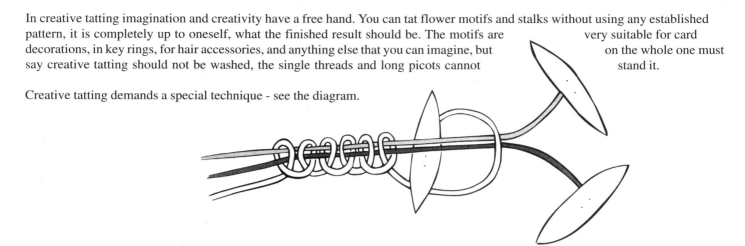

You can tat with several tatting shuttles at the same time. The stalk between the flowers is tatted using reverse knots, that is to say that it is the thread from the tatting shuttle in the right hand, which makes the knots, see fig 13 pages 10. When the stalk is the desired length, tat the leaves and flowers with the required shuttle.
Flowers and leaves are tatted with ordinary double stitches or with Josephine knots.
The leaves can for example be single rings, several rings together or trefoils. The flowers can be placed singly or several at the same place.
The picots can be few or many, short or long, closed or cut open.
The thread in the shuttles can have different thickness and colour likewise. You can also use different qualities of thread just remember the thread should be smooth, firm and strong if you want to pull the knots together to form a ring. Creative tatting is started and finished with a frayed knot. If you tat single flowers it will be clumsy to use frayed knots, and it is not necessary. If the motif is to be glued on to a card for example the end of the thread should be cut close to the ring, it won't open.
On page 51 there is a detailed visual pattern of a motif for a place card. It is a good idea to start to tat this motif to enable you to practice the technique. On page 49 you can see six different examples of cards. On page 52 you can see examples of motifs for key rings, candle guards and hair band. For all motifs on page 49 we have used DMC no. 80 in different colours. The motifs 1,2,5 and 6 are started with single coloured stalks and afterwards gathered together with the green stalks and leaves. On no. 1,2 small beads are glued on as stamens.
On no. 610 small golden beads are glued on. Arrange the motifs on the cards and glue them firmly.
For all the key ring-motifs on page 52 we have used DMC no 80 in different colours and for the hair band and the candle guard DMC no. 8 was used. For the candle guard you tat around a curtain ring, which is 3.5 cm in diameter, see page 24. Afterwards you tat a stalk in red and green. At the same time an extra green thread runs inside on which you have golden beads.
On each stalk between the groups of flowers you tat 2-3 reverse knots, a golden bead is pulled forward and again you tat 2-3 reverse knots before the next group of flowers. When the stalk is long enough the ends are tied in bows and the wreath is sewn on the curtain ring with sewing thread.

Motif for place card

Materials: 3 shuttles
     1 place card
Thread: DMC Special Dentelles in white, blue and green
Size: the stalk is app. 5 cm long

Tat the stalk as shown on the diagram. Start and end with a frayed knot.
Glue the stalk on the place card.

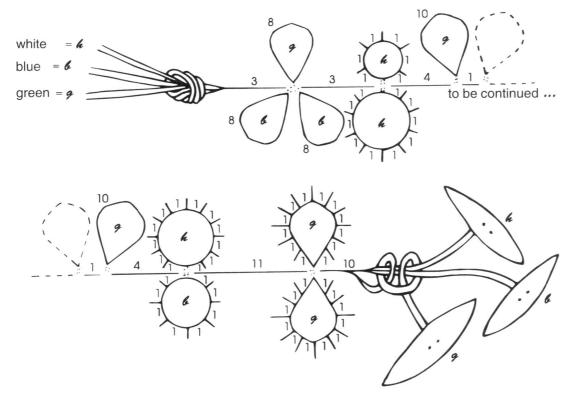

white = *h*
blue = *b*
green = *g*

to be continued ...

51

Four-leaf clover for key ring

Materials: 1 shuttle + ball thread
                     1 key ring with plastic pendant 4 cm in diameter
Thread: DMC Cordonnet Special No. 40, colour 320 green
Size: 3 cm in diameter

Place a paper clip at the start of the work.
Tat the leaves as chains and join in the space made with the paper clips.
After the last leaf continue with the tatted spiral string as stalk. Finish with a frayed knot and cut the ends.

Earring

Materials: 1 shuttle
                 a fine crochet hook
                 2 large rings 4 cm in diameter
                 1 pair of earring wires or clips
Thread: DMC Cordonnet Special No. 40, colour 3326 pink

First tat the centre motif. Finish with a frayed knot.
Crochet around the ring, joining to the motif at the same time. Start with 2 double crochet around the ring at the closing point. The third double crochet is joined to a picot and then carry on as usual. There are 7 double crochet between each picot joining. Finish with 2 double crochet after the last picot. Fix the ends with a needle before cutting them off.

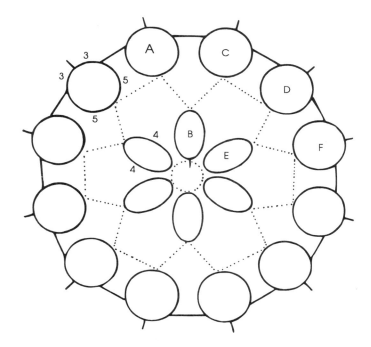

54

How to work hemstitch

Pull 2 threads out of the fabric where the hemstitch is to be worked.

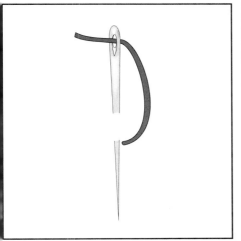

figure 1 : Sew around 3 threads from the pulled section.

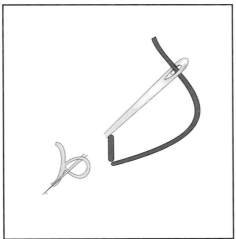

figure 2: Sew around 3 threads in the fabric and through the picot.

figure 3: Repeat the sewing through the picot.

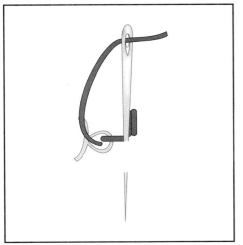

figure 4: Sew around 3 threads from the pulled section.

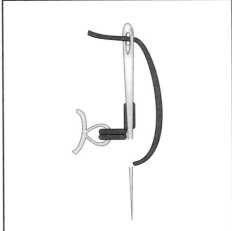

figure. 5: Repeat the sewing around the 3 threads.

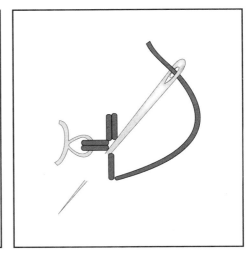

figure 6: Sew around 3 threads in the fabric.